Ellen Ochoa's Journey t⬚ : A Bedtime Story abou⬚ ⬚ne First Hispanic Woman in Space

By Cody Dragon

<u>DEDICATION</u>

I dedicate this book to my daughter Alyssa - you've changed my life in ways you'll never know. Remember, the view is always better when you take the high road.

Once upon a starry night,
In a land far, far away,

There lived a girl named Ellen Ochoa,
who dreamed of flying
high one day.

She loved science and
outer space,

and the way the moon would shine
down on her face.

Ellen would love to look up at the stars in the sky,

She spent her days in wonder,

saying "My, oh my!"

One day, when Ellen was grown,
she learned of a place so grand,

Where people flew to space,
to explore new lands.

Ellen Ochoa's Journey to the Moon

She worked and studied hard, until one day when she finally reached her goal.

She was going to outerspace and perhaps take a stroll

In the milky way or perhaps
on the moon

Ellen Ochoa had done what
so many thought
she couldn't do.

Ellen Ochoa's Journey to the Moon

Now Ellen flies among the stars,
soaring high through the sky.

She's a shining example,
of what we can achieve if we try.

So when you're tucked in bed tonight,
And the stars are shining bright,

Remember Ellen's journey
and let your dreams take flight.

THE
END

Ellen Ochoa's Journey to the Moon

THE
END

Printed in Great Britain
by Amazon